wild, wild world
WILD CATS
AND OTHER DANGEROUS PREDATORS

Written by
Clare Oliver

Illustrated by
Ross Watton

p

This is a Parragon Publishing Book
This edition printed for Books Are Fun in 2001

Parragon Publishing
Queen Street House
4 Queen Street
Bath BA1 1HE, UK

Produced by

David West ☂ Children's Books
7 Princeton Court
55 Felsham Road
Putney
London SW15 1AZ, UK

British Library Cataloguing-in-Publication Data

A catalogue record for this book is available from
the British Library.

Hardback: ISBN 0-75254-682-1
Paperback: ISBN 0-75255-619-3

Printed in Italy

Designers
Jenny Skelly
Aarti Parmar
Illustrators
Ross Watton
(SGA)
Rob Shone
Cartoonist
Peter Wilks
(SGA)
Editor
James Pickering
Consultant
Steve Parker

CONTENTS

4 What do cats, dogs and bears have in common?

5 What is a Tasmanian devil?

5 Are hyenas dogs?

6 Do dogs ever kill people?

7 When do bears eat people?

7 Are there killer cats?

8 Do lions hunt alone?

8 How loud is a lion's roar?

9 Do lion cubs look like their parents?

10 Can any animal outrun a cheetah?

11 How does the cheetah kill its prey?

11 Where do cheetah cubs live?

12 Who's the biggest cat of all?

12 How big is a tiger's paw?

13 How many tigers are there?

14 Which leopard has lost its spots?

14 Who hides in the trees?

15 Who hides a feast in the trees?

16 How can you tell small cats from big?

16 Which cat barks?

17 Which cat has the most kittens?

18 Do hyenas laugh?

19 Do hyena cubs get on together?

19 Do hyenas hunt?

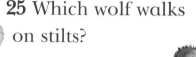

20 How do dogs hunt?

20 Do dogs use babysitters?

21 What do pups eat?

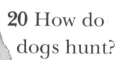

22 What changes coat in the winter?

22 Who's at home in the city?

23 Who won the race, the fox or the hare?

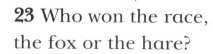

24 Which is the biggest dog?

25 Do wolves howl at the Moon?

25 Which wolf walks on stilts?

26 Which is the biggest bear?

27 Which cubs drinks the creamiest milk?

27 Can bears walk on water?

28 Which bear fishes for its supper?

28 When do bears climb trees?

29 Do all bears eat meat?

30 Where can you see bears close-up?

31 How do dogs help people?

31 Where can you see big cats close-up?

32 Glossary & Index

Grizzly bear

4

What do cats, dogs and bears have in common?

They are all mammals. This means that they are covered with cozy fur and feed their young with mother's milk. Cats, dogs and bears are also all carnivores, which means they eat meat. To do this, they have special sharp, pointy teeth, called canines.

Is it true?
Cats, dogs and bears are the only carnivores in the world.

No. Many other mammals, such as hyenas, weasels, raccoons and humans eat meat. So do other animals – birds of prey, some reptiles and sharks in the sea.

Great white shark

[?] What is a Tasmanian devil?

The Tasmanian devil lives in Tasmania, an island south of mainland Australia, and belongs to the same mammal family as kangaroos, carrying its babies in a pouch on its tummy. It's small, ferocious, and can defend itself well against other predators.

Tasmanian devil

[?] Are hyenas dogs?

No, though they look quite similar. Hyenas hunt in packs like dogs, but they have four toes per foot, whereas dogs have five on their front paws. Hyenas are not cats either, but are closely related.

❓ Do dogs ever kill people?

The gray wolf is one member of the dog family that is powerful enough to kill a person. There have been tales of gray wolf attacks in Europe and Asia. The worst story dates back to 1948, when a pack appeared in Darovskoye, Russia. Witnesses said the wolves killed 40 children and then disappeared, probably with very full tummies!

Amazing! Stories such as *Goldilocks*, *Little Red Riding Hood* and *Peter and the Wolf* were probably made up to stop children from wandering off into places where there were dangerous bears and wolves.

Gray wolves

Indian tiger

Is it true?
Foxes are more dangerous than wolves.

Yes. Although foxes are too small to attack a person, they are far more dangerous because they can carry a deadly disease called rabies. A bite from a rabid fox could mean death for the victim unless he or she reaches a doctor in time to be given anti-rabies medicine.

? When do bears eat people?

When they're very, very hungry polar bears! Bears usually avoid people, but occasionally young male polar bears attack people, during especially harsh winters.

Grizzly bear

Bear Country

Danger do not Approach or Feed

? Are there killer cats?

Cougars, jaguars and leopards have all killed people, but the serious maneaters are lions and tigers. One tigress was said to gobble up 436 people in just eight years!

Amazing! Lions doze for up to 20 hours a day. They save all their energy for hunting and fighting.

? Do lions hunt alone?

Most cats are loners, but lions hunt as a team with the rest of their pride (family group). Male lions are too easy to spot with their huge flowing manes, so usually the females hunt. Still, the male lions get to dig into their share first.

Lioness

Lion

? How loud is a lion's roar?

Very loud! On a still day, and it usually is quite still in Africa, a lion's roar can be heard three miles away. Lions roar to show other lions how strong they are, and to communicate with other members of the pride.

Yes and no. Normally, only male lions have manes. A mane makes them look bigger and scarier, and the extra fur protects their neck in a fight. Lionesses do not usually have manes, but people studying lions in Africa have come across a few females with mini manes of their own!

Wildebeest

9

Lion cubs

Do lion cubs look like their parents?

Adult lions have plain, sandy-colored fur, but their cubs have spots on their coats. This might be camouflage, to make them difficult to see when their mother has to leave them alone and go off hunting.

? Can any animal outrun a cheetah?

Over short distances, the cheetah tops 60 miles per hour, and no animal can beat that. Cheetahs reach such high speeds partly because their dog-like claws work like running shoes and give them a good grip. But the speed king soon runs out of puff. If an impala keeps ahead for more than 550 yards, its life is saved – at least this time!

Impala

Cheetah

Amazing! The average cheetah hunt is over in seconds! A cheetah may spend hours lazing about lying in wait, but it normally runs down its prey within 300 yards. It takes the cat less than 20 seconds to catch its meal!

Cheetah with prey

How does the cheetah kill its prey?

The cheetah lives on the African grasslands. It usually chases animals such as antelopes, gazelles, or even ostriches. When it catches up with its fast-running prey, it fells and kills it by clamping its strong jaws on to its neck.

 **Is it true?**
Cheetahs are spotted all over.

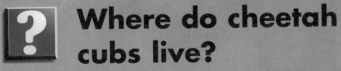

No. The cheetah is mostly spotted, but its tail is striped. And the king cheetah, which is extremely rare, has stripes on its back where the spots have joined up.

Where do cheetah cubs live?

Cheetah mothers don't have a permanent den. Instead, they move their cubs around a couple of times each week. This stops other big cats finding and preying on them.

Cheetah and cub

11

Is it true?

Tigers don't attack a victim which looks them in the eye.

Yes. Tigers usually attack from behind. In Southeast Asia, people sometimes wear masks that act as fake faces, on the backs of their heads.

Siberian tiger

? Who's the biggest cat of all?

The Siberian tiger can grow to be nearly eleven feet long – that's about six times longer than a pet cat. This tiger is very rare and lives in the mountains of northern China and Russia. Its long, off-white, striped fur keeps it warm and hidden in the snow.

12

? How big is a tiger's paw?

Huge – almost as big as a grownup's head! Even a gentle swipe of its paw would easily knock you off your feet.

Amazing! The cub of a male tiger and a female lion is called a tigon. Lions and tigers are so closely related that they have been bred together in zoos. Ligers are the cubs of a female tiger and a male lion.

? How many tigers are there?

There are five main types of tiger – the Siberian, South Chinese, Sumatran, Indochinese and Indian. The number of tigers has fallen faster than for any other cat. There are fewer than 5,000 in the world today.

Caspian tiger (probably extinct)

? Which leopard has lost its spots?

The black panther, which is really a type of leopard! But if you were brave, or foolish, enough to get close to a panther, you'd see faint spots in its fur.

? Who hides in the trees?

Lots of spotted cats, including leopards and jaguars, hide in the trees to take a nap or lie in wait for their prey. The dappled light through the leaves makes everything look spotted, so their coats are the perfect camouflage.

Leopard

Leopard

Amazing! The snow leopard is a champion long-jumper! This rare big cat can clear a 50 foot-wide ditch – that's over one and a half times further than the human long-jump record.

Who hides a feast in the trees?

Sometimes leopards kill such big prey, that they can't eat it all in one go. Leopards can drag a whole deer up into the branches of a tree, safe from jackals and hyenas, which can't climb up and steal it!

15

Jaguar swimming

Is it true?
All cats hate the water.

No. Quite a few types of cat enjoy a swim. Jaguars in the South American rainforests often bathe in the River Amazon. They love to snack on river turtles and sometimes even kill crocodiles!

? How can you tell small cats from big?

Most big cats – lions, tigers, jaguars and leopards, roar. Small cats can only purr. There are lots of types of small cat, all over the world. They include the pet-cat-sized leopard cat of southern Asia, and the jaguarundi and ocelot, which both live in North and South America.

Caracal

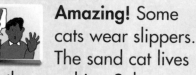

Amazing! Some cats wear slippers. The sand cat lives in the scorching Sahara Desert in Africa. It has special, thick pads on its paws to stop them from being burnt on the hot sand, during the day.

European wild cat

Caracal

? Which cat barks?

The caracal sounds more like a dog than a cat, because it barks when it wants to call its mate. It also has tall, tufted ears, a short tail and can even be trained as a hunting pet. It is famous for leaping to catch birds in mid-air.

Jaguar

European wild cat

Ocelot

Jaguarundi

Leopard cat

? Which cat has the most kittens?

Most small cats have between one and four kittens at a time, but the European wild cat has litters of as many as eight kittens! This champion breeder is found all over mainland Europe and also lives in the Highlands of northern Scotland.

17

Is it true?
Wild cats can breed with pet cats.

Yes. But many pet cats are too scared to let their wild cousins get close enough! European wild cats often breed with pet cats or strays. The pedigree Bengal is a cross between a leopard cat and a tabby.

? Do hyenas laugh?

The spotted, or laughing, hyena has two different calls. One sounds like a laugh, but the other sounds more like a wail. This hyena is very daring. It has attacked sleeping people and has even carried off young children!

Amazing! Hyenas work as garbage collectors. Hyenas are scavengers – they will eat just about anything. In some African villages hyenas are sometimes allowed in to clear the trash.

Spotted hyenas

Is it true?
All hyenas have manes.

No. Spotted hyenas don't, but striped hyenas and brown hyenas do. They have scruffy-looking hair sticking up around their head and even down their back.

18

? Do hyena cubs get on together?

Hyena cubs play with each other to practise the skills they'll need as adults, but they don't really get on. Twins fight over food, and sometimes, the weaker twin slowly starves to death.

Hyena cubs

Vultures

Lioness with prey

? Do hyenas hunt?

Spotted hyenas do, but other hyenas prefer other animals to do the work for them! Most hyenas feed mainly on carrion, which is a bigger hunter's leftovers. When they do hunt for themselves, hyenas go for wildebeest, zebra, or they steal a goat or cow from the local farmer.

❓ How do dogs hunt?

Many dogs, including African wild dogs, hunt in groups called packs. First they spread out, so they have a good view of the landscape, then they close in on their prey. They keep in contact with barks and body language.

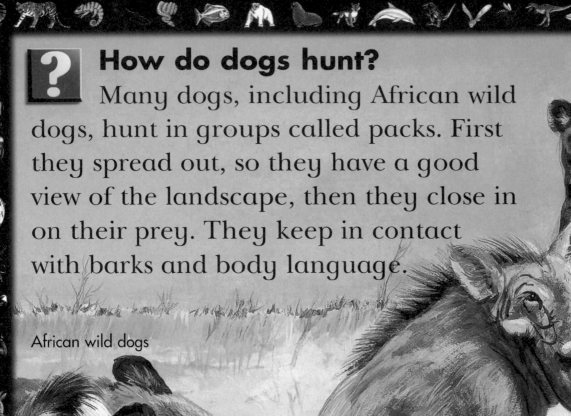

African wild dogs

Warthog

❓ Do dogs use babysitters?

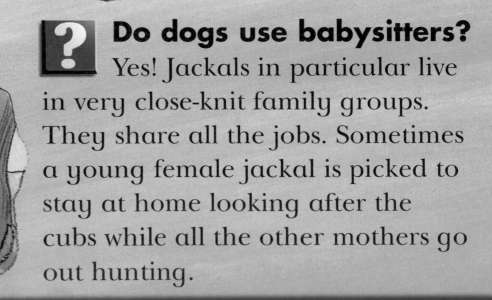

Yes! Jackals in particular live in very close-knit family groups. They share all the jobs. Sometimes a young female jackal is picked to stay at home looking after the cubs while all the other mothers go out hunting.

Is it true?
Dogs have five toes on each front paw.

Yes. But the African wild dog is the one exception. This fierce hunter is missing a toe on each front foot.

African wild dog pups

Amazing! Dogs can't sweat! Unlike you, dogs don't have sweat glands, so they can't lose heat through their skin. They pant when they get hot, to let heat escape from their bodies.

Saint Bernard

? What do pups eat?
Newborn wild pups live off mother's milk. Soon, their mom brings them meat. She chews it for them, until they're a bit bigger. Finally at four months old, the pups are old enough to join in the hunt.

? What changes its coat in the winter?

The Arctic fox lives in the far North. In the summer, when flowers are in bloom, its fur is reddish brown. During the icy winter, it turns snowy-white for camouflage.

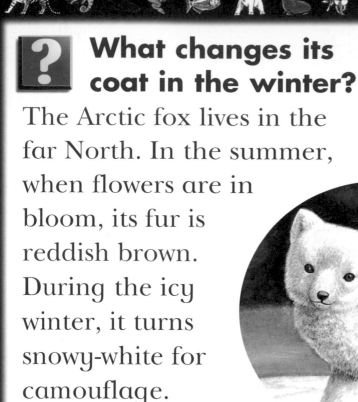

Arctic fox

 Is it true?
Fennec foxes have huge ears.

Yes. In fact, they're six inches long! Fennecs hunt at night so they need good hearing to find prey. Big ears also help their body heat to escape.

? Who's at home in the city?

Fantastic Mr Fox! The red fox is just as happy in the town as in the countryside. At night, it goes through trash cans looking for tasty morsels or catches rats.

22

Gray fox

Amazing! The gray fox can climb trees! From high in the branches, the fox gets a good lookout for rabbits and mice. It can also grab a fast-food snack, such as fruit or an egg from a nest.

City foxes

? **Who won the race, the fox or the hare?**

Foxes only catch hares by creeping up quietly and not being seen. If the hare hears or sees the fox, it dashes off. Hares can outrun foxes, and both animals know it!

? Which is the biggest dog?

The gray wolf is biggest wild dog and the most powerful. Males can be well over six feet long and weigh 175 pounds, as much as four six-year-old children! Some gray wolves have brown, red or black coats.

Gray wolf

Amazing!
Except for the African wild dog, all pet dogs are descended from a wolf-like ancestor, which appeared about one million years ago.

? Do wolves howl at the Moon?

Wolves howl whether the Moon's out or not. They use their powerful voices to tell other packs of wolves to stay away, and to talk to members of their own pack, especially when they have spread out to hunt.

? Which wolf walks on stilts?

The maned wolf is the tallest wild dog. Its legs are longer than the length of its body! The maned wolf lives in the grasslands of South America. Its stilts give it a good view over the tall Pampas grasses.

 Is it true?
You should never try to stare down a wolf.

No. You should if you're a musk ox. Wolves usually hunt by picking off young or sick members of a group of grazing animals. Musk oxen try to stop this happening by huddling in a tight circle. Faced with a wall of horns, the Arctic wolves can't pick off any individual oxen.

Maned wolf

? Which is the biggest bear?

The powerful polar bear weighs in at 1,320 pounds, which makes it about ten times heavier than a grown-up person, and the biggest of all meat-eating land mammals. Adult bears snack on fish and seals, but they have even been spotted guzzling down fat beluga whales that weigh as much as themselves!

Polar bear

Amazing! Polar bears cover their nose with their paw when they hunt. Although their fur is white, their noses are black and easy to spot in the snow. By covering its nose, the polar bear makes sure that its whole body is camouflaged against the snowy Arctic landscape.

Which cubs drink the creamiest milk?

Newborn polar bear cubs are tiny. They need to fatten up quickly to survive the cold. Luckily, their mother's milk is thick and creamy and about half of it is pure fat.

Polar bear cubs

Can bears walk on water?

They can when it's frozen! Polar bears roam across northern Europe, northern Asia and North America. If the Arctic Ocean isn't frozen they swim, protected by thick fur and fat!

Is it true?
Polar bears poisoned Arctic explorers.

Yes. Polar bears' livers contain a lot of Vitamin A. In small doses, this is fine for humans, but when hungry explorers ate the livers, they were poisoned.

? Which bear fishes for its supper?

The brown bear is a top angler. It knows just the time of year that delicious salmon head upriver to lay their eggs. The bear catches the fish with a quick swipe of the paw, or it waits until the salmon leap up mini waterfalls, and become tired.

Brown bear

Brown bear cub

? When do bears climb trees?

When they want to escape danger. Black bears are expert climbers even as grown-ups. Brown bears only climb trees when they are cubs, usually to escape from adult brown bears, who are trying to eat them!

Amazing! The American black bear is one of the world's champion snoozers. Its winter sleep, or hibernation, lasts for seven months – over half of the year!

 Is it true?
Koalas are bears.

No. Although we call them koala bears, koalas are really marsupials, which means they have pouches like kangaroos. Pandas aren't bears either. They're more closely related to raccoons.

 **Do all bears eat meat?**
Even meat-eating bears sometimes like a change of diet. Polar bears snack on seaweed and berries when seals are scarce. Brown and black bears love honey, but collecting it is a very risky business. They often come away from the hive with a stung nose!

29

Giant panda

American national park

❓ Where can you see bears close-up?

National parks give bears a home where they're safe from hunters. If you visit one of these nature reserves, remember that bears are wild and can be dangerous to humans.

Huskies pulling sled

Amazing! Pet owners live longer! Lots of people choose to share their lives with pet cats and dogs, the cousins of wild lions and wolves. Stroking an animal feels good and helps pet owners to relax. Scientists think this may explain why they live longer.

? How do dogs help people?

Lots of dogs work for us. Huskies pull people around in the icy Arctic. Other dogs' jobs include mountain rescue, herding sheep and helping blind and deaf people. The skills which wild dogs use to hunt, such as working as a team and having superb senses, make them ideal for these tasks.

Is it true?
Humans are the most dangerous animals on Earth.

Yes. Animals which attack humans are extremely rare, but we have hunted animals for fur, and destroyed their habitats. That's why so many creatures are in danger of dying out.

? Where can you see big cats close-up?

In a zoo. Some people think it's cruel to keep animals away from the wild. Other people say that zoos are useful for breeding rare cats and teaching us about them.

Lions in zoo

Glossary

Bear Family of carnivores including brown bears, polar bears and grizzly bears.

Canines The pointy teeth in a carnivore's jaw, used for tearing into flesh.

Carnivore Any mammal, or other animal, which has teeth adapted for eating meat.

Carrion The dead body of an animal.

Cat Family of carnivores divided into big cats that roar (lions, tigers, jaguars and leopards) and small cats that purr.

Dog Family of carnivores including wolves, foxes and jackals.

Habitat The type of place where an animal lives in the wild. The polar bear's habitat is the icy Arctic.

Mammal A warm-blooded animal which gives birth to live young and feeds its babies on mother's milk.

Marsupial A mammal that gives birth to very undeveloped live young, that live at first in their mother's pouch.

Litter Baby animals born from the same mother at the same time.

Pedigree A domestic (not wild) animal that has been bred to have certain characteristics.

Predator An animal that hunts other animals for food.

Prey An animal that is hunted by another animal for food.

Pride A group of lions who live together.

Index

African wild dog 20, 21, 24
Arctic fox 22
Arctic wolf 25

babies 4, 9, 11, 17, 19, 20, 21, 27
bear 4, 6, 7, 26–29
black bear 28, 29
brown bear 28, 29

camouflage 9, 12, 14
canine 4
caracal 16
carnivore 4
carrion 19
cat 4, 5, 7, 8–17, 30
cheetah 10–11
communication 8, 16, 18, 20, 25
cougar 7

dinosaurs 5
dog 4, 5, 6, 7, 20–25, 30, 31

European wild cat 16, 17

fennec fox 22
food and hunting 4, 5, 8, 10, 11, 15, 16, 19, 20, 21, 22, 23, 25, 26, 27, 28, 29
fox 7, 22–23

gray fox 23
gray wolf 6, 24
grizzly bear 7

hyena 4, 5, 15, 18–19

jackal 15, 20
jaguar 7, 14, 15, 16
jaguarundi 16, 17

leopard 7, 14–15, 16, 17
leopard cat 16, 17
lion 7, 8–9, 13, 16, 19, 30

mammal 4

maned wolf 25
maneaters 6–7, 18
marsupial 5, 29

national park 30

panda 29
pets 17, 30
polar bear 7, 26–27, 29
prey 10, 11, 12, 14, 15

rabies 7
red fox 22

sand cat 16

Tasmanian devil 5
tiger 7, 12–13, 16

wolf 6, 24–25, 30
working dogs 31

zalambdalestes 5
zoo 13, 31